# HORSES
# AND RIDING

# Contents

Published in 1986 by Warwick Press
387 Park Avenue South, New York 10016
First published in 1986 by Kingfisher Books Limited,
a Grisewood & Dempsey Company
© Piper Books Limited 1986
Printed by Printer Portuguesa, Portugal

5 4 3 2

ISBN: 0-531-19021-8
Library of Congress Catalog Card No. 85-52382

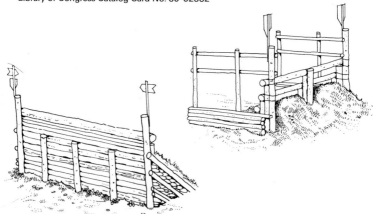

# HORSES
## AND RIDING

by
Georgie Henschel

Editor: Alan Wakeford
Designer: Ben White

A Gateway Fact Book
Warwick Press
New York/London/Toronto/Sydney
1986

# The Story of the Horse

The horses and ponies which you see around today have changed a great deal over the years. The story of the horse began some 60 to 40 million years ago. There lived then a creature called *Eohippus*. This animal walked on toes rather than hooves. It had four toes on each front leg and three toes on each hind leg. One of the most important changes was the way in which these toes turned into hooves. As time went by, the legs with four toes also became three-toed. Gradually, the middle toe strengthened. The side toes no longer touched the ground and a hoof started to form. These early horse-like animals had a bone structure very similar to the first primitive horse, called *Equus Caballus*. However, there were some differences. The neck had grown longer and the shape of the head and jaw had changed. It had also grown strong chewing muscles in its lower jaw and the upper jaw had become smaller. This allowed room for a larger brain.

Left: The first horse, called *Eohippus*, was a small animal about the size of a fox. It walked on toes rather than hooves.

Below: *Eohippus* grew and changed through the ages. The bones of its legs became like those of today's horse, and the toes became hooves.

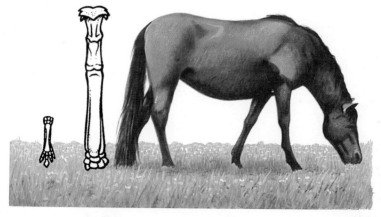

7

# The Horse's Ancestors

Changes in climate caused these early horses to develop into different types and colors. One of these early horses was the Tarpan. It roamed wild in eastern Europe and western Russia. The Tarpan is now **extinct**, but scientists are sure it is one of the modern horse's ancestors. In Poland today there are two native pony breeds, the Hucul and the Konik, which are very like the Tarpan. Przewalski's Horse (named after the 19th-century Russian explorer Professor N. M. Prze-walski) was once thought to have been an ancestor of the horse. These days scientists consider it to be a completely different species.

The **equine** family has three branches: *Equus Caballus* is the horse branch, *Equus Hemiones* is the donkey branch, and *Equus Zebra* is the zebra branch. A jack (male donkey) bred to a **mare** (female horse) will produce a mule. A **stallion** (male horse) and a jenny (female donkey) will produce a hinny. But neither the mule nor the hinny can reproduce.

**Below: Przewalski's Horse.**

## The Ice Age

During the Great Ice Age, which occurred millions of years ago, much of the earth's surface was covered with sheets of ice. It was at this time that *Equus Caballus* first appeared.

The severe cold forced many animals in the Northern Hemisphere to move south. Eventually the ice retreated and the climate became warmer. Grass began to grow on the bare Arctic **tundra** and forests started to spring up. The horses which had moved south in Europe and Asia now began to spread out onto the tundra and into the forests. They developed according to the different climates in which they found themselves. A mild climate tended to breed larger horses. A severe

Above: Primitive drawing of a horse found in a cave in France.

climate gave rise to ponies rather than horses.

Because of this, there were several types of *Equus Caballus* at the end of the Ice Age. Primitive cave drawings in France show sturdy ponies as well as heavier horses (known these days as draft horses). Cave drawings in Spain, on the other hand, show horses of a much finer, Oriental type.

Horse fossils dating from before the Ice Age have been found in the Americas. But strangely, there is no evidence that horses existed there after the ice retreated.

9

# Horses in the Wild

No one knows when, or in which part of the world, the horse was first **domesticated** (tamed by humans). We do know that for thousands of years horses lived as wild animals in herds. They were hunted for food by many animals and probably also by people. The horses relied on the alertness of the herd leader and their own speed to survive.

All domesticated horses still like a certain amount of freedom loose in a field. By watching them there we can learn a lot about them. Horses enjoy the company of other horses. They like being able to use their physical energy and high spirits as they would in the wild. Horses will spend hours galloping, rolling, bucking and playing together. In the wild, they work out an order of importance within the herd. This can also happen among the domesticated animals.

The horse has now been man's servant and friend for more than 3,000 years. Yet it still has the instincts of a wild animal. It is suspicious of the unknown or unexpected and flees from anything frightening or painful.

The horse, like all **herbivores**, is not a fighter by nature. Unlike the **carnivores**, a horse will only attack another creature in self defense. It will kick or bite if it is being cruelly treated or if it feels cornered.

**Above: In the wild, the horse is a herd animal and relies on the herd leader for its well-being. Even today it gallops away from danger, which may seem surprising, given its size.**

## Survival

Survival in the wild was made easier for the horse in two ways. First, all horses have sharp hearing. Secondly, they have widely spaced eyes which give them both side vision and rear vision. But the horse's field of vision

**Above: The horse has only a narrow line of bifocal sight but it sees well to the side and quite far to the rear.**

**Above: The ears of a horse are sensitive and it can rotate them to pick up sounds.**

using both eyes is far narrower than ours. In order to see an object with both eyes, it has to turn its head and look directly at it.

It is important to remember these facts when handling horses. They should be treated calmly but firmly. As their hearing is sharper than ours, they should never be shouted at. They can recognize different tones of voice, and can be taught to understand words in the same way that a dog can. The position of their eyes explains why they sometimes **shy** at something we cannot see, because it is out of our line of vision. Horses that respect their human handlers seem to trust them in the same way that they used to trust their herd leader in the wild. Horses have different personalities in the same way that people do. But very few are vicious by nature. It is usually when they are frightened or unsure of their rider that they behave badly.

11

## Domestic Horses

Confident, well-mannered adult horses can usually be handled quite safely even by young children. Many ponies seem to have a special liking for children, and will look after their young riders.

When a horse has complete confidence in its rider, it can perform extremely athletic feats. Some horses have greater ability than others. But few would attempt the types of jumps involved in show jumping or horse trials on their own. Horses are generous animals and it is important not to ask too much of them. This is especially true when they are young, as their bones are not fully developed. One of the most important things to remember is that ponies get bored just like people. So try not to make them tired of jumping by doing too much at once.

**Below: Horses and ponies are friendly animals. If they are well trained, they can be handled safely by small children.**

# After the Ice Age

At the end of the Ice Age, there were four main types of *Equus Caballus*. The Celtic or Atlantic Ponies were small animals which did not move very far south. Instead, they adapted themselves to harsh climates and lack of vegetation. The Exmoor Pony is one of the oldest breeds, and the nearest in type to its primitive ancestors. The second type includes the North European and North Asian Forest Horse. These horses lived on the rich vegetation of the tundra or in the humid climate of the fast-spreading forests. They were bigger animals and ancestors of the heavy draft horse. The third type was the Eastern, or Oriental Horse. These horses from Central Asia developed quite differently from those in colder climates. This was probably because they were not forced by the ice to change their habitat. Finally, there was the Miniature Horse of Western Asia which is thought to have been an ancestor of the Arab.

**Exmoor**  **Akhal-Teke**

**Friesian**  **Caspian**

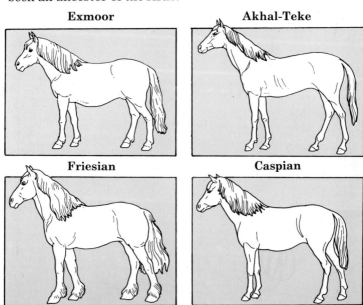

# Crossbreeding

Once horses were domesticated, people began to realize that by crossbreeding different types, they could produce animals useful for certain jobs. This is how breeds were first established.

A number of different types of heavy horse were bred from the North European Forest Horse. The largest and strongest were bred to carry knights in full armor into battle. They were also used for **jousting**, where the weight they had to carry was around 420lb (190kg). The medieval Great Horses of England were used for this sport. They were animals of great bulk and strength. On the continent of Europe, one of the horses they used was the Schleswig Heavy Draft Horse, still popular in Germany. The English Shire, which is descended from those ancient Great Horses, is the largest draft horse in

**Below: Until the tractor was invented, farmers used the horse to help cultivate the land.**

the world today. In the old days, heavy breeds were also used to pull coaches and carriages over the rough and uneven roads of the time. For work on the land, smaller, but strong, horses were more effective.

## The French Breeds

The French bred some excellent light draft breeds for work on the land. They were active enough to be used as saddle and army horses as well. These breeds include the Ardennais, the Breton and the Comtois. Later, they evolved the Percheron, which were bigger but very lively. Their strength allowed them to pull coaches and carriages at quite a speed.

## The Oriental Horse

Many horses and ponies were crossed with the Oriental horse to produce animals that were fast and bold. Early riders were often warriors, so wars and invasions

were responsible for much crossbreeding. The winning side would often steal the best of the enemy's horses and leave their own behind. This is just one of the ways breeds came to be established. Oriental horses have always been the aristocrats of the equine world. A very ancient and much prized Oriental breed is the Akhal-Teke, of Russia.

**Right: In the Middle Ages, horses and riders both wore armor, not only for battle but also for the knightly sport of jousting. Horses had to be strong because armored riders were very heavy.**

## Arab and Barb Blood

Another ancient French draft breed is the Boulonnais. This breed is unusual in that it contains blood from two hot-blooded breeds, Arab and Barb. They were brought back to France by Crusaders. This combination produced horses which could run very fast. Before the days of refrigerated transport, they were used to take loads of fish from the coast of France to Paris.

**Above: When cavalry fighting became more active, horses had to be trained in many advanced dressage movements.**

## The Friesian

Each country concentrated on breeding draft horses with the qualities needed for its particular types of work. The "Low Countries", which consisted of what is now Belgium and the Netherlands, were fortunate to have a type of Forest Horse which was able to do all kinds of work. As a breed it has remained more or less unchanged for some 1,000 years. It is called the Friesian Horse.

The blood of this breed has helped in the formation of many other draft, and later, carriage horse breeds. The "Flemish" stallions were imported into many countries all over the world. They were the ancestors of the Friesian Horse of today.

## The Riding Horse

As time passed, armor became lighter, and fighting on horseback became more a matter of skill and precision than weight and brute force. Lighter and more athletic horses were needed. A suitable type of horse was found in Spain. The breed, known as the Andalusian, was developed by the Carthusian monks. They crossed native mares with Oriental stallions brought into the country by the Moors. For a long time the nobility thought of the Andalusian as the finest riding horse in Europe. Their lovely paces and kind temperaments encouraged riders in the 16th and 17th centuries to study the "art of equitation" seriously.

16

## Riding Schools

Riding schools were built in many European cities and riding masters wrote books explaining their methods. There was a new interest in the long neglected art of equitation. Many breeding farms sought to produce better quality, more athletic horses. As well as importing Arabs and Barbs, they brought in Andalusians from Spain. Their blood helped to found one of the best-known breeds in the world today, the Lipizzaner.

Above: The Andalusian.

Below: A Lipizzaner performing the "levade" in the Spanish Riding School in Vienna.

## Criollos

Horses were reintroduced to the Americas by the Spanish Conquistadores. Therefore, they were either pure or part-bred Andalusians. A strange future was in store for many of them. When the Indians sacked Buenos Aires and turned out the Spaniards, the horses were driven out onto the **pampas**. There they lived and bred in the wild for 300 years. Only the strongest survived the harsh conditions which forced them to struggle for their lives. They adapted themselves in size and coloring to their surroundings. These wild horses of the pampas came to be known as Criollos. They are well known for their high level of endurance. A famous example of this took place in the late 1920s when Professor Tschiffely rode 10,000 miles (16,000 km) from Buenos Aires to Washington using only two of these extraordinary Criollos.

**Below: The Criollo is a tough breed of small horse native to South America. It is descended from Spanish horses which were taken to the continent in the 16th century.**

## The Arab

The Arab is the oldest pure breed in the world. It has the blood of no other breed in its veins. Because of this, its own character is passed on to any other breed it may be crossed with. This is called absolute dominance. Its blood has helped to found many light horse breeds. Three Arab stallions were the founding fathers of the world's most valuable and fastest horse, the Thoroughbred.

Today horses are divided into three groups: "hot bloods" (Arabs, Thoroughbreds, Anglo-Arabs, and the Akhal-Teke of Russia); "cold bloods" (work and draft hor-

**Above: The Arab is the oldest pure breed in the world. It is a horse that combines beauty with strength, endurance and a kindly temperament. Arab blood has led to the improvement and establishment of many light horse breeds. Three Arab stallions were the founding fathers of the world's most prized breed, the Thoroughbred.**

ses); and "warm bloods" (a mixture of the two). The majority of riding, driving and competition horses are "warm bloods" with varying degrees of "hot blood" in their makeup.

Above: Native ponies grow thick coats in winter. They have long manes, forelocks, and tails, which keep them warm in winter and keep off flies in summer.

# Ponies

Ponies do not come into the horse groupings. This is not just because they are smaller – 57 in. (145 cm or 14.2 hh) and under. (1 hh or "hand" is equivalent to 4 in. or 10 cm). They are also different from horses because they have spent a longer time fending for themselves in the wild. This means that certain parts of their body have developed to help them to cope with harsh climates and poor feeding. They are deep-bodied and shorter in the leg than horses. The **cannon bone** is short and they have very good **bone**. This gives them great strength for their size. It means they are able to carry much more weight than if they were just "little horses."

Pony breeds differ as much as horse breeds do, but all have some common characteristics. For instance, they all have well-shaped heads with wide-set, intelligent eyes. Their **muzzles** are broad (but tapering) and their nostrils can swell out surprisingly far.

## Living Conditions

Ponies seem to have a more independent nature than horses. They have grown used to looking after themselves through the centuries. When domesticated, they enjoy stables as cosy places to come to for feeds. But they mostly prefer to live outside, even in winter. They have tough constitutions and can keep in good health on relatively less food than horses. This is because their metabolism (the rate at which their bodies turn food into nourishment) is different.

They are renowned for their "sure-footedness," which means they are steady on their feet and rarely stumble. This feature is left over from the days when they lived wild. Britain has nine breeds of native (correctly known as Mountain and Moorland) ponies ranging in height from 35 in. (89 cm or 9 hh) to 57 in. (145 cm or 14.2 hh). But today, the native ponies of Norway, Iceland and Austria are almost as well known.

**Below: Highland Ponies living in freedom on the Island of Rhum, off the west coast of Scotland. The liver chestnut color with light mane and tail is characteristic.**

# British Breeds

Both the smallest and the largest British ponies are Scottish. The Shetland is never more than 40 in. (102 cm or 10 hh), and for its size it is the strongest of all equines. The Highland Pony can vary from 52 in. (130 cm or 13 hh) to 57 in. (145 cm or 14.2 hh). The two largest English breeds are the Dales and the Fell. The Connemara is a native of Ireland but it is very popular and bred in many countries. The original pony of Wales is the one now known as the Welsh Mountain Pony. From this come the Welsh Riding Pony, the Welsh Pony of **cob** type, and the big Welsh Cobs. The New Forest Pony originates in southern England and is very popular abroad. Throughout history, so many different stallions have bred in the Forest that New Forests vary a great deal in height and type. Dartmoor and Exmoor Ponies are good for small children because they are not only small at 49 in. (125 cm or 12.2 hh) but also narrow, which makes them easier for short legs. The Celtic Pony is an ancestor to all native pony breeds.

New Forest

Welsh Mountain

Dartmoor

Shetland

Exmoor

# The Horse's Body

Horses and ponies have the same basic *conformation*. This is the word used to describe all the points, or parts, of the horse's body. But each breed has its own characteristics because particular parts of the body have developed differently. For example, the Shire and the Thoroughbred are horses of completely opposite types. One is bred for strength and great pulling power. The other is built for high speed. Both have the same points. But the sum of those points (or their conformation) could hardly be more different. Even so, a Shire with the good points of its breed will be just as well-proportioned and nice to look at as a good Thoroughbred. In most English-speaking countries, horses are still measured in hands. The measurement is taken from the highest point of the **withers** to the ground.

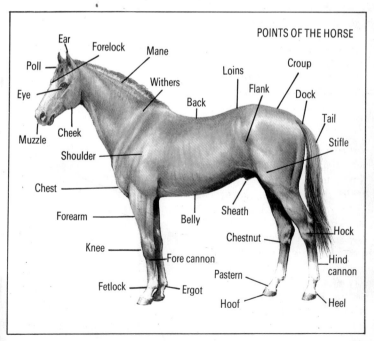

POINTS OF THE HORSE

Ear
Forelock
Mane
Poll
Loins
Croup
Eye
Withers
Flank
Dock
Back
Tail
Muzzle
Cheek
Stifle
Shoulder
Chest
Forearm
Belly
Sheath
Knee
Chestnut
Hock
Fore cannon
Hind cannon
Fetlock
Ergot
Pastern
Hoof
Heel

Brown

Palomino

Black

Cream

Dun

# Colors

The five basic colors are bay, brown, chestnut, black, and dun. Gray, and the many mixed coat colorings, are caused by pigmentation variation. A gray horse must have had one gray parent and all grays grow lighter

with age. A bay horse has a black mane and tail, and black legs, usually from the knee and **hock** down. A brown horse has a brown mane, tail and legs.

Chestnuts can vary from dark liver to rich gold: they never have black legs, mane or tail. A black horse must have a black muzzle (the

Chestnut

Strawberry Roan

Bay

Piebald

Skewbald

Gray

muzzle is brown on dark brown horses).

There are many shades of dun: gray, yellow, fox, mouse and cream. All duns carry the **dorsal stripe**, and many have zebra markings on the legs. Gray duns tend to grow lighter with age and if they do, the dorsal stripe fades. Roan horses have white hairs flecked through their coats. There are three shades of roan: strawberry, bay, and blue. A piebald is black and white and a skewbald is brown and white, or brown, black and white. Palominos are golden with silvery mane and tail. The three Appaloosa coat patterns are blanket, leopard, and snowflake.

25

## HEAD MARKINGS

| Star | Snip | Stripe | Blaze | White face |

## Markings

Today, all competition and show horses have to have vaccination certificates and registration papers. For these it is necessary to know how to describe the various markings which they have on their heads and legs. A white mark on the forehead is always called a "star," even if it is not exactly star shaped. A white line running down the face is a "stripe." If the stripe runs down from a star, it is called a "star and stripe." A broad band of white running from forehead down to muzzle is a "blaze." If the white spreads out around the eyes and to the sides of the face, it is a "white face." A small white mark on the muzzle is a "snip."

Some horses, particularly chestnuts, have hairless pink patches on their muzzles or lips; these are called "flesh marks." A white patch anywhere else on the body is simply described as a "white patch." Leg markings are

## LEG MARKINGS

| Stocking | Sock | Fetlock | Pastern | Coronet |

equally simple. White stretching right up the leg, often on the inside, is a "full stocking." If it stretches to the knee or hock, it is a "stocking" and if it stretches halfway up the cannon it is a "sock." White covering the **fetlock** joint is a "white fetlock" and white covering the **pastern** only is a "white pastern." A narrow circle of white around the **coronet** is a "white coronet."

## Teeth

Horses, like humans, have two sets of teeth: the temporary "milk teeth" are gradually replaced by permanent teeth. The front teeth, which are used for cutting, or grazing, are called **incisors**. The back teeth, used for chewing food, are **molars**. Between the two is a gap called the "bars of the mouth" where the bit lies. Horses have three pairs of incisors. Foals are sometimes born with the central pair just coming through. By the time they are two, they will have all three pairs. These are gradually replaced by the permanent ones, a pair at a time, with the central pair first.

When a horse is five, it has all three pairs of incisors. This stage is called having a "full mouth."

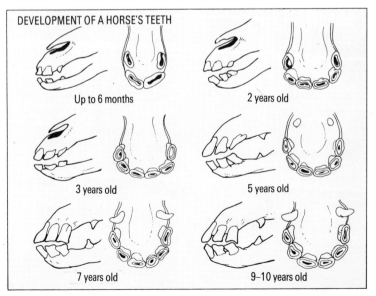

DEVELOPMENT OF A HORSE'S TEETH

Up to 6 months

2 years old

3 years old

5 years old

7 years old

9–10 years old

# Horses at Work

The horse was first put to work by man as a pack animal. Members of wandering tribes used them for carrying belongings from place to place. Until fairly recently, they were still used in this way. The Fell and Dales Ponies of Northern England carried weights of up to 225 lb (102 kg) in the lead mines. Before wheels were invented, people built sled-like carts on runners for horses to pull. It must have been all right on flat ground but awkward and very uncomfortable up and down hills and on rough ground.

**Above: Horses and ponies have been used as pack animals for as long as they have been working for people. The pony here is carrying baskets of lead ore from a mine in England in the 1700s.**

The horse has been of most value to us in farming the land. Until machines such as tractors were invented, horses were used for all farm work. In mountainous districts, however, hardier native ponies were used instead of horses for this sort of work.

## Farm Horses

The horse was used in farm work for every job from spreading manure, plowing, harrowing, sowing, and reaping, to bringing in the harvest. Some farms still make use of workhorses for various tasks.

Many ranchers nowadays use jeeps and trucks for overseeing work and surveying their land. However, on the big sheep and cattle stations of Australia, the *estancias* of South America, and the ranches of the U.S., horses are still used for herding and roping.

**Above: In the western United States and Canada, horses are still used on cattle ranches for herding and for steer and calf roping. They also feature in rodeos, where they demonstrate their skill. Many are Quarter Horses. In Australia, horses are used on big sheep farms, called *stations*.**

## Brewery Horses

In parts of Europe, breweries still use heavy horses to pull their delivery carts. These beautifully turned-out horses are a welcome sight in cities in this mechanical age.

## The Police Horse

These days, the truest working partnership of man and horse is, perhaps, that of the mounted policeman. Police horses are bought young, trained with great skill and patience, and finally paired with a suitable rider. Once paired, they stay together for the horse's working life, or for as long as the policeman works. In Britain, the different branches of the mounted police run a number of varied competitions each year. The competitions end in the Horse of the Year Show. The winner of this will become the proud rider of the "Police Horse of the Year."

The horses are superbly trained and the policemen, whom you probably only ever see calmly walking the streets on their mounts, are excellent riders. One of the most exciting displays performed by the Mounted Police is the Musical Ride. But perhaps the most romantic police force in the world is the Royal Canadian Mounted Police, "The Mounties." They were formed in 1873 to police about 300,000 square miles (800,000 sq. km) of cold, often snow-bound Northern Territory. Their record is one of great courage and of hardship endured by both man and horse. Although they no longer work on horseback, the Mounties keep their horses for ceremonial occasions and for their Musical Ride. They are still brilliant horsemen.

**Below: Mounted policemen like this one are often seen in city streets.**

## Ceremonial Displays

In Britain, the pageantry of the horse is an important part of state ceremonies. The Queen's coach makes quite a spectacle drawn by a magnificently harnessed team of Windsor Greys. The coach-

**Above: The Drum horses and the Band of the Household Cavalry of Britain in full dress. They appear in this finery on ceremonial occasions or when presenting their Musical Ride. Notice the beautiful saddlecloths and the highly polished drums.**

men and postilions complete the spectacular scene with their traditional colorful uniforms. Although cavalry is no longer used in active warfare, some countries have preserved units for show. In Britain this is the Household Cavalry. There are two regiments, the Blues and the Royals, and they share alternate guard duty at Buckingham Palace. These units also give displays of quadrilles and musical rides at horse shows at home and abroad. There is also a mounted branch of the Royal Horse Artillery called the King's Troop. It gives exciting displays of fast and accurate gun carriage maneuvers. France has preserved the *Garde Républicaine*. It is military in origin, but now serves as a civilian mounted police force. When giving performances of its Musical Ride, the riders wear their traditional scarlet and gold military uniforms. For similar ceremonial purposes, Spain preserves the *Gardia Civile*.

31

# Horses for Sport

## Flat Racing

Thoroughbred racing is carried on today in about 50 countries. King Charles II established Newmarket as the headquarters of racing in Britain, which it has remained ever since. The official governing body of the sport is the Jockey Club, founded in 1750. Jockey Club Stewards attend all race meetings to make sure that they are "run to rule." Many races are **handicap** ones. In these, the weights carried by the different horses are decided upon by the Jockey Club's official handicapper. The Classics are races for three-year-olds. The horses run at level weights. That is, all **colts** carry 126 lb (57 kg) and **fillies** carry 119 lb (54 kg). The British Classics are the 2,000 Guineas (colts), and the 1,000 Guineas (fillies) at Newmarket, the Derby (both sexes), the Oaks (fillies) at Epsom, and the St. Leger (both sexes) at Doncaster. The races are run at progressive distances of 1 mile, $1\frac{1}{2}$ miles and $1\frac{3}{4}$ miles.

The first Derby was run in Britain in 1750. Most countries have their own series of Classics. In Europe and the United States, there are also important races for three-year-olds and upward. The saddle and bridle are included in the weight a horse has to carry, which is why racing saddles and irons are small and light.

Below left: Flat racing. The field is still spread out; who is going to win?

Below: The winner of a race is being escorted to the unsaddling enclosure by two mounted policemen, so that enthusiastic crowds do not upset it.

Above: A jockey has to "weigh in" before and after every race. The saddle and bridle are included in the weight a horse is to carry, so they must be light.

## Steeplechasing and Hurdling

Steeplechasing is so called because the first recorded cross-country race was a match between two Irishmen who raced their horses from "Buttevant Church to St. Leger Steeple." The sport soon became popular in England as well as in Ireland. It eventually became officially known as National Hunt Racing. The greatest steeplechase, the Aintree Grand National, was first run in 1839, and won by a horse called *Lottery*. Another classic British steeplechase is the Cheltenham Gold Cup, which is run in March. Great

**Above: Steeplechasing is a sport for bold horses and brave riders, especially when they are jumping bunched up together like this. Steeplechase jockeys are professionals. Both men and women compete together these days.**

chasers achieve wide popularity.

Hurdle racing is run over obstacles which slope slightly away from the oncoming field. For this reason, they can be jumped faster than steeplechase fences. The British hurdle classic is the Waterford Crystal Champion Hurdle which is held at Cheltenham in March.

## Hunting

The hunting of wild animals, whether mounted or on foot, is one of the oldest sports. In the past, it was practiced by the ancient Chinese, Egyptians, and Greeks. Fox-hunting is its most recent form, but in the Middle Ages, people hunted the wild boar, the stag and the fallow deer. This was mostly through forests, where there was little or no jumping. At the end of the 17th century, when forests began to be cleared and fields enclosed, the fox soon became the most hunted animal. Hounds could run fast across open grassland. To keep up, the followers rode on horseback, jumping over boundary fences, hedges, stone walls and even wide brooks. Gradually, the famous hunts of England and Ireland were established. Hunting also takes place in the United States, in Virginia, Maryland, and other states as well. In New Zealand, there are no foxes, so they hunt the hare. In France, they hunt the hare, the wild boar, and the deer.

**Below: The master, his huntsmen, and "whipper-in" move off to draw the first covert after the meet. Many people these days regard hunting as a cruel pastime. Others say that it is a far less cruel way of controlling the fox population than poison, snaring or trapping.**

# The Three Day Event

The Three Day Event is one of the hardest tests for both horse and rider. Every year, more and more people compete in novice and intermediate One Day Events but only the most talented riders and the best horses reach the top of the tree. The Three Day Event consists of three stages: **dressage**, speed and endurance, and show jumping. Dressage is ridden on the first day. Next comes speed and endurance which itself is in three parts: roads and tracks, steeplechase, and cross-country. Show jumping is on the third day.

**Above: Two straightforward cross-country jumps. Note the direction arrows.**

To produce a horse calm enough to perform a dressage test, fit enough to complete the speed and endurance tests and sound enough at the end to complete a course of show jumps is quite an achievement. It is a test not only of horsemanship but also of horse management.

The Three Day Event started as a military exercise, and was first recognized as an official equestrian sport at the 1912 Olympics. Badminton, in England, is now the most important Three Day Event in the international calender. It was first held in 1949. In 1961 an autumn Three Day Event was started at Burghley, also in England. Like Badminton, it is now a place where important international championships are held.

## Eventing Today

Today, many countries stage international Three Day Events. The official title of these is *Concours Complet Internationale* (CCI). Among famous names in the Three Day Event world are Sheila

Willcox of Britain, who won Badminton three times running; Bill Roycroft of Australia, who was the first person to ride three horses around Badminton; and Lorna Sutherland (now Lorna Clarke) of Britain. Shortly after, it was ruled that no one could ride more than two horses. Mary Gordon-Watson of Britain, Bruce Davidson of the United States, Mark Todd of New Zealand, Mark Phillips, Richard Meade and Virginia Holgate of Britain are also among the leaders in their field. British rider Lucinda Green's astonishing record of six Badminton wins on six different horses is probably unbeatable.

Three Day Event jumps probably look more frightening to the spectators than to the riders. A well-designed course is meant to test, rather than terrify, the competitors. Today, many successful riders reach the top by starting in the Junior and Young Riders competitions. "Eventing" is probably the British riders' favorite sport, perhaps because of the long tradition of riding to hounds in that country.

**Below: Eventing, or riding in Horse Trials is one of the most popular equestrian sports. Large crowds turn out to see the top riders.**

# Pony and Riding Club Horse Trials

Eventing is not the sort of sport which you can walk into at the deep end. From a pony club upward there are horse trials to suit all abilities. These are called One Day Events and they are organized by pony clubs and riding clubs. Official ones, for Juniors, Young Riders, and Adults are highly organized. One Day Events are run at different levels: novice, intermediate and advanced.

The One Day Event consists of three phases: dressage, show jumping and cross-country, (no roads and tracks or steeplechase).

Dressage is always ridden first, show jumping is usually next, and cross-country last. Every year, pony club branches in each area organize inter-branch competitions.

**Below: A nice cross-country jump. The pony is wearing boots and overreach boots on its forelegs for support and protection.**

The winners qualify for the championships. Riding clubs also organize inter-club qualifying competitions. Prizewinners go on to compete for riding club championships.

**Above: These five pony club children are at camp. They are going out to practice for the Prince Philip Cup Games of Britain. Notice their distinctive shirts. In competitions, each branch wears its own colors.**

### Starting to Compete

To start riding in a pony club or riding club horse trial you need a well-schooled, obedient pony or horse. You also need to be an experienced rider. The One Day Event, like the Three Day Event, is a test of both riding ability and horse or pony management. For dressage and show jumping, riders wear formal riding clothes. For cross-country, riders usually wear a colored sweatshirt and a **skull cap** with matching **silks**.

For dressage, the horse or pony must wear neither bandages nor a **martingale**. Pony clubbers are allowed a **pelham** but everyone else at novice level must use a **snaffle**. Tack should be carefully checked before setting out cross-country. Also, it is very important to walk the course paying attention, not only to the jumps, but also to the direction flags. You can be disqualified for missing them, or for going around them the wrong way!

39

# Show jumping

In all countries, show jumping began as a military sport. At the beginning of this century, there were jumping competitions at many big horse shows, but at that stage nobody had established a jumping "style." The officers still used the old hunting seat (forward on the takeoff and back when landing). It was an Italian cavalry officer, Federico Caprilli (1868–1908), who originated the forward, or balanced, jumping seat which is practiced by show jumpers today. His method spread through the cavalry schools of Europe.

Another Italian, Colonel Paul Rodzianko, had studied with Caprilli and brought his teaching to Britain. One of his pupils was Colonel (then Major) Mike Ansell, who did much to raise the level of British show jumping after World War II.

The oldest show jumping center in England was established at Olympia, a stadium in London, in 1907. The Christmas show here is renowned for its special atmosphere. Lady Wright was the

SHOW-RING JUMPS

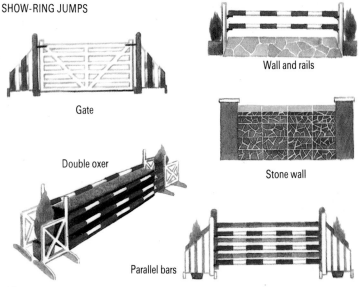

Gate

Wall and rails

Double oxer

Stone wall

Parallel bars

first woman to make a name for herself in show jumping at Olympia before World War I.

## Learning to Show jump

Although show jumping looks relatively easy when performed by experts, it is essential to be a good rider first. Jumping is fun and riders often want to try it long before they are capable of doing so without causing discomfort to their ponies. But not everyone who enjoys riding wants to jump. The little logs and ditches to be found on a country ride are sufficient for many. If this applies to you, do not feel that you have to learn to jump because that is what all your friends are doing! On the other hand, if you want to jump and you have the talent and the nerve, pay attention to everything instructors may tell you. Watch and try to learn from the top riders you see on television. There are no shortcuts to becoming even a moderately good show jumping rider.

**Above: This horse is jumping happily with ears pricked while the rider is allowing it to stretch its head and neck.** It is wearing overreach boots, tendon boots, a plain snaffle bridle and rubber bit-guards.

**Great Names in Show Jumping**

After World War I, so many civilians, both men and women, started to take up show jumping that it became obvious it was going to become an important international sport. In 1921, the *Fédération Equestre Internationale* (FEI) was formed in France to make rules which would apply to all international competitions. In the same year, Lt. Colonel Geoffrey Brooke became the first British winner of the highly valued King George V Cup. Only three riders (all British) have won this cup three times: Captain Talbot Ponsonby, Colonel Harry Llewellyn (each time on *Foxhunter*), and David Broome.

In the 1950s and 1960s

Above: This is the grand finale of the Horse of the Year Show in Britain, when all the prizewinners come into the arena together.

there were many successful British women riders, the greatest of whom was Pat Smythe. She was the first woman to jump in the Olympics (in 1956) on her horse *Flanagan*. In more recent years, an equally brilliant rider was the late Caroline Bradley. The most remarkable partnership of the 1960s was that of Marion Mould (then Coaker), and *Stroller*, who stood 57 in. (145 cm or 14.2hh). Together they won the Queen Elizabeth Cup and the first Women's World Championship ever held. They went on to win three Hickstead Derbies and the

Individual Silver at the Mexico Olympics.

These days, winter is spent preparing for shows in indoor schools and entering qualifying competitions for the Volvo World Cup final in Spring. Great names past and present in the world of show jumping include Hans Gunther Winkler of Germany, the d'Inzeo brothers of Italy, Bill Steinkraus of the United States, Hugo Simon of Austria, and in Britain, Nick Skelton, the Whitakers, Liz Edgar – and Harvey Smith and David Broome who were show jumping before many rising stars were born!

Show jumping today is an expensive sport which means that few private individuals are rich enough to enter it seriously. Fortunately, it is such a major attraction that sponsors have become interested. They help by providing money for the individual riders and by offering prizes for competitions.

## Children's Show Jumping

A jumping pony which has won on many occasions for someone else will not necessarily win for you. To be a good show jumper, you must be a good all-round rider. This means lessons, and hard work. Your pony cannot do its best until you have a firm seat which works without the help of your hands. Without this you are likely to jab its mouth and probably bump its back on landing. Or you may hang onto the reins on takeoff and tip your weight so far forward that the pony can neither stretch its neck and head nor lift its forehead. In children's jumping classes it is often the child who stops the pony rather than the pony which refuses. An old saying tells us not to "run before we can walk." In riding, try not to jump until you ride well enough to help, rather than hinder, your pony.

**Below: A refusal is not always the pony's fault.**

# Polo

Polo is a very old equestrian sport which is said to have started in Persia 2,000 years ago. The British discovered it in India, where it had been played for centuries on small, strong, native ponies of about 53in. (135cm or 13.2hh). In 1869, cavalry officers brought the game to England. They increased the pony height to 56in. (142cm or 14hh) then in 1896 increased it again to 57in. (145cm or 14.2hh). In 1919, this height limit was abolished. Today, most polo ponies are, in fact, horses. This has not really improved the standard of the game. Originally, teams consisted of nine players. As ponies got bigger and faster this was reduced first to seven and then to the present four.

Polo was introduced to the United States in 1876 and quickly spread to South America. Argentina soon produced both top class players and highly prized ponies. Polo became popular in England between the two world wars. After World War II, it might have died out had it not been for the enthusiasm of Lord Cowdray, Prince Philip, and the late Lord Louis Mountbatten.

Polo is played in chukkas of seven and a half minutes each. There can be four, six, seven or eight chukkas, and there is always a five minute break at half time.

**Left: For polo, ponies wear boots or bandages and the rider also protects his knees with kneepads.**

# Dressage

Everyone who rides in a One Day Event has to ride a dressage test. Dressage is a French word which comes from the verb *dresser* meaning to "train up, to make straight, to direct." So riding a dressage test simply means showing the judge that you have trained your horse or pony correctly. It must move straight and obey your directions, or your **aids**.

Any well-trained horse or pony should be able to perform a preliminary or novice test quite easily. All a basic test really consists of is a halt and salute, then a series of simple movements at walk, trot and canter.

Dressage at the higher levels is very disciplined. As the movements asked for become more difficult, the performance of a test by a good rider becomes more like a demonstration of the "art of equitation."

**Below: Dressage can start at any age. This young girl is riding her skewbald pony very nicely at a working trot. Note, in particular, the way in which she is looking up and sitting straight.**

## Serious Dressage

Dressage specialists ride in a particularly deep-seated saddle. It has a high **pommel** and **cantle**, long straight panels, and long girth straps, buckling onto short leather girths. In dressage, judges award marks for each movement. These range from 0 (movement not performed) up to 10. At the top level, which is the Grand Prix, the movements become those of the High School. The most difficult of these include the **piaffe**, the **passage** and the canter **pirouette**. Dr. Reiner

**Above: The highest level of all: Olympic Gold Medalist, Dr. Reiner Klimke is riding *Ahlerich* perfectly balanced in the passage.**

Klimke, riding *Ahlerich*, won the Gold Medal at the 1984 Olympics. Chris Bartle, on *Wily Trout*, finished sixth. This was the highest placing ever achieved by a British rider at the Olympics. Liz Hartel of Denmark was a well-known woman rider who won two Olympic Silvers, even though she had polio.

# Long Distance Riding

Organized long distance riding is becoming very popular in many countries. It is suitable for all ages of rider, and for all breeds and sizes of horse and pony. Some rides run by the official equestrian organization of the country concerned are of 100 miles (160 km) or more.

In Britain, rides are organized by the British Horse Society's Long Distance Riding Group and by the Horse and Pony Endurance Society. The Golden Horseshoe is the most important long distance ride.

On all competitive rides, where distances have to be covered in specific times, there are stops for veterinary checks.

Long distance riding is still very much an amateur sport. It is not expensive because you do not need a special horse or pony (although you do need to know a lot about horse management if your mount is going to complete the distance successfully).

The sport is also a good way of exploring a new country. One way of trying it is to go on a riding holiday to a center which organizes day

**Above: Ready for a country ride using a "general purpose saddle" (below), suitable for hacking, jumping, or cross-country work.**

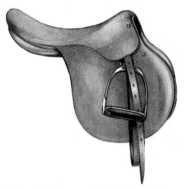

rides. It is a good idea to go to one recommended by either the equestrian body or the tourist association of the country you have chosen.

47

# Harness Racing

Trotting races were popular in many parts of the world before there were any organized equestrian sports. Farmers and country people tested their horses and ponies against one another in matches. In Britain, the Norfolk Roadster was a particularly good trotting breed. On the continent, the Friesian Horse of North Holland was commonly used. The Hackney was bred from the Roadster (which had Arab and Thoroughbred blood). There is also Roadster blood in the French Trotter, a breed which is almost as highly prized as the Standardbred of the United States in the harness racing world. The Standardbred itself, although mainly Thoroughbred, had some Friesian blood in the early days from mares which were imported by Dutch settlers. The Friesian also contributed to the Orlov Trotter, the famous Russian harness racehorse. In fact, many Orlov Trotters today are black, the color of their Friesian ancestors.

Harness racing takes place in most European countries, in the USSR, and in Australia and New Zealand. It is in the United States, however, that the sport is most highly organized. Harness race meetings are often held in the evening by floodlight.

**Below: Harness racing is an exciting sport. These horses are trotting. The second one is about to try to pass the first. Notice the protective boots and bandages which prevent the horses from injuring their legs.**

## Pacing

Some harness race horses trot and some pace. Pacing is when the hind and foreleg of the same side swing forward together. Pacers wear a special type of harness which prevents them from falling back into the normal, diagonal trot. They achieve a slightly faster time than trotters and the two race separately. In France, French Trotters are raced both in harness and under saddle. The United States may be the foremost harness

**Above: Harness racehorse trotting. Racing vehicles are very light.**

racing country today, but the sport first became officially recognized in Russia. The Orlov Trotter competed in Moscow as early as 1799.

# Driving

Long ago, before the motor car was invented, horse driving was a necessity. Today, perhaps because people welcome a rest from machines, it is becoming popular again. Many people are taking it up as a hobby and some, more ambitiously, as a sport. Most well-behaved horses and ponies that have been **broken to saddle**, can be taught to go in harness.

The first step is to help them get used to wearing a driving harness and a bridle with blinkers. Then they should be long-reined in the harness and finally taught to pull a weight. This is often a heavy pole attached by chains or ropes to the collar or breastplate. The first vehicle to be pulled should be an exercise cart with long shafts. The horse may be

Above: Training for the driving pony starts with lunging. Then the pony is long-reined wearing a bridle. Next it is trained to pull a weight. Finally, it is put to an exercise cart, and then to a proper vehicle.

upset at this stage by the sound of the wheels which seem to chase it from behind. Once the horse is used to the cart, a helper is needed to hold the animal while the trainer gets on board. For the first few times, the trainer will probably be glad to have someone leading the horse while he or she concentrates on driving.

In the driving world, the person who drives is called the "whip." Many people, when they have learned to drive, want to test their skill against other whips. They start by driving a *single*,

driving trials. In Britain, the official trials are organized by the British Driving Society. In these there are novice and open competitions. The successful novices graduate to the open. In each section there are classes for singles, pairs, teams of four horses, and tandems. For each class there is a yearly National Championship.

that is, one horse or pony. Showing classes are popular starting points in competing. Then, as they improve their skills, whips soon want to try their hand at competitive

**Below: This young boy in a Governess cart is driving a beautifully turned out Shetland Pony.**

# Learning to Ride

No one can learn to ride from a book but here is some good advice and facts to remember. First, never forget that balance is more important than grip. If you are in balance with your pony, your body will accept the movement of its paces under you. To achieve this, try not to be tense, and try to get to know and feel the rhythm of those paces. The walk is in four time, the trot is in two time, and the canter in three time. You use your seat and legs to ask the pony to go forward and your hands, which are the controls, should be sympathetic. You will not be a good rider until you have an independent seat, and to help with this, you must learn to ride without thinking of the reins as lifelines. The better you ride, the more comfortable it will be for your pony, and consequently the better it will go for you. If it is possible, go to a good riding school and have as many lessons as you can afford. Remember that the best riders in the world say that they go on learning all their lives!

Left: Mounting. Below: The walk in four time, then the trot in two time followed by the canter in three time. Finally, the gallop, which is

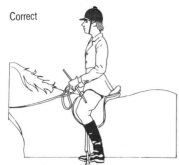

Correct

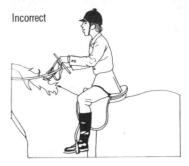

Incorrect

## Position

The position of the rider in the saddle is very important for good riding. There are a number of things to remember when trying to achieve a good position. First, you must sit in the deepest part of the saddle with head up, shoulders wide, and the inside of your thigh laid softly

**Above: In the correct position, the rider sits nicely in balance. Note the line from shoulders through seat to heel.**

against the saddle. Your knee joint should be relaxed and your lower leg close to the pony's side. Carry rather than hold the reins.

**also in four time because each leg touches the ground separately. Right: Swing the right leg over the horse's back.**

## The First Step

The best way to start riding is on the **lunge**. It is hard trying to remember everything at once. On the lunge, the instructor controls the pony. This means that you do not have to worry about where it is going and can concentrate on balance and developing your seat. Sit squarely in the deepest part of the saddle. Look up and keep your head upright and shoulders relaxed. Your thighs should be against the saddle, but do not try to hold the saddle with them. Relax your knee joints and allow your lower leg to hang down naturally from the knee. Take the stirrup with the ball of your foot and let your ankle feel supple. The sole of your foot should always be parallel to the ground. If you sit comfortably in balance, your shoulders, hips, and heels should be in line and so should your knees and toes. You will probably be asked to do exercises which will help you gain confidence and make you supple. Learners can sometimes be nervous when they start and this makes them stiff, tense, and unbalanced.

**Below: Lunging is a good way to develop your seat, balance, and confidence. It is also fun when you can do exercises. Many experienced riders like to be worked on the lunge from time to time.**

## Riding Lessons

When you have riding lessons, make sure that you pay attention to your instructor at all times. Teachers at good riding schools know that you may be nervous at first. If you are, do not be afraid to admit it. If there is anything you do not quite understand, ask your teacher.

When you have learned to canter and ride **school figures** (with and without your stirrups), then you will start learning to jump. At first you will learn to walk or trot over poles on the ground. Do not think that this is too easy to bother about. The exercise helps ponies and horses to approach jumps calmly and accurately. Also, it helps you to accept the stronger forward movement under you. You learn to

**Above: This lesson is taking place in an indoor riding school. It is one of the best ways of learning to ride, so if there is one near you, try and go to it. It is a good idea to go and watch a class first so that you know what to expect.**

allow for this with your hands, and to go forward from the hips without leaving the saddle. Soon there will be a small jump at the end of the poles. Gradually, if all goes well, you and the pony will soon be jumping a course of small, varied jumps. Once, you can jump, do not allow yourself to forget about working on the flat. This will still improve your riding, and the better you ride, the better your pony will jump!

55

# Clothes

It is not necessary to have a complete riding outfit when you go for your first lesson. Your first, basic need is a riding hat or skull cap. Riding schools do rent hats, but it is best to have your own. It is important that it should fit you exactly. You also need sensible footwear. Jodhpur boots are a good buy as you will wear them even when you have the complete outfit.

At first make do with low-heeled (not platform soled) lace-up walking shoes. It is better to start riding in shoes or jodhpur boots than rubber riding boots which will make your legs feel stiff and heavy. Also, until you are over 16, it is correct to wear jodhpur boots when showing or competing. Eventually you may be able to afford a pair of real leather riding boots.

You will get rubbed sore if you start riding in jeans, especially if they are too tight. Corduroy or wool trousers are more comfortable until you buy jodhpurs. You will find it easier to mount, (and you will look better from behind), if they are not absolutely skin tight. Until you show or compete it is

**For informal riding, anything goes provided you have a hat, sensible shoes or jodhpur boots and comfortable trousers.**

sensible to buy dark colored jodhpurs: brown or navy.

For lessons or informal riding, it is perfectly all right to wear anything neat, warm, or waterproof on your top half over a shirt or sweater. Black jackets are only for shows and formal riding. A tweed hacking jacket is warmer and more practical. Make sure that any jacket

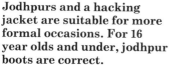

Jodhpurs and a hacking jacket are suitable for more formal occasions. For 16 year olds and under, jodhpur boots are correct.

Dressed for cross-country. Skull cap with silk and matching shirt. Number bib, jodhpurs (or breeches) and boots.

feels comfortable across the back and around the armholes. It is sensible to buy it big enough to allow you to wear a sweater underneath in cold weather.

For cross-country, you should wear a brightly colored striped sweatshirt. If it is cold, you can put a light woolen sweater under it. If you or your mother can knit, a woolen shirt is very cozy. But remember that whatever the weather, you will get hot riding! Also, the reason for wearing distinctively-colored shirts and silks is to help the commentators and the spectators to recognize who is who. You should also wear gloves: it is sensible to take two pairs in case it rains.

**Left: Good mounting picture of a rider just ready to spring up. Try to land lightly on your pony's back. Above: A child's safety stirrup.**

# Clubs

If there is a pony club branch near where you live and you are under 21 it is a good idea to join. As well as learning a great deal, you may also enjoy meeting other pony enthusiasts. If you do not yet have a pony of your own, you could perhaps hire one from your local riding school, or borrow one from a friend. Pony clubs have regular teaching rallies and many branches also run a yearly camp.

Pony clubs run a series of tests which are graded as follows: D is very easy, C is when you are getting better

and B means that you are a good rider. A is the final grade which few pony clubbers achieve. When you pass each stage you get a special colored button to wear. Most branches hold competitions in which their own members compete against other branch members. In this way, the pony club finds qualifiers for the various pony club championships.

Once you are 17 or over, you can join a riding club which runs activities similar to those of pony clubs. They also run teaching rallies and competitions. Some are for their own members and some are open ones. Clubs also like their teams to qualify and compete for the annual riding club championships. Riding clubs' progressive grade tests will encourage you to improve both your riding and your knowledge of horse care and management.

Pony and riding clubs run enjoyable social activities. Lectures, discussions, stable-management demonstrations, quiz competitions, and annual dinners are some of the entertainments. They also organize inexpensive outings to interesting places. Famous farms or important horse shows are some of the places you could visit with your club.

**Below: These children are at a pony rally. They are practicing their jumping over a course of small obstacles.**

Pony and riding club competitions are run in classes to suit riders' ages and abilities. Young children on small ponies have simple courses, jumps, and dressage tests. Novice adults (and horses) have novice courses, jumps and Preliminary or Novice dressage tests. Riders who do well at this level move up to the intermediate level. Many top riders started their careers in the pony club. Organizers always need helpers; so if you are not riding one day, why not offer to help as a jump judge, a steward or even as a mounted runner?

# A Horse of Your Own

If your pony is going to live outdoors (and only native ponies are able to do this all year round) you need a well-fenced field and a secure gate (padlocked if you live near a big town). If there is no running water, get a trough and keep it clean and full. Your pony also needs either a field shelter or a stable in which it can be fed and groomed. This is also essential as a place to rest if the pony becomes lame or ill.

The easiest way to keep a horse or pony is to use the "combined" system. This means that in summer it will be stabled by day (or part day) and out at night. In winter it will be in at night and out by day. A stall should be big enough for the animal to move about freely and to lie down in comfort. This requires a space of 12′ × 12′ (3.6m × 3.6m) for horses and 10′ × 10′ (3m × 3m) for ponies. The door should be in two halves with two bolts on the bottom half. The top half should be left open in any weather apart from a blizzard or gale. The floor should be made of roughened concrete or brick. A slight slope toward the front is better for drainage than a center drain.

Above: The top door of a stall should always be left open except in wild storms so that the horse can see what goes on in the yard.

Above: A nice roomy field shelter with a hay rack on the wall inside. Build these with their backs to the prevailing wind.

**Stable equipment. Left to right: pitchfork, wheelbarrow, bucket, fork, broom, shovel, vermin-proof container for feeds, measuring scoop, and rubber pan for feeding.**

## Looking After Your Horse

In order to keep the stall and yard clean you will need a wheelbarrow, a stable broom, a shovel, and a fork. You will also need a pitchfork for shaking the straw when you muck out and for laying a bed. It is a good idea to sprinkle the floor of the stall with a watered-down disinfectant from time to time. In winter, a field shelter should have a straw bed as it encourages ponies to lie down. It should be kept clean of droppings. To feed the animal in the shelter you can either fix up a rack or attach a hay net to a tie ring.

It is wasteful to feed hay on the ground. A shelter can be used as a stall if about one third of the front is walled. You will need a good solid water bucket for your horse or pony. When setting it down, make sure that the handle is to the back, away from the horse. A feed pan or basin, and a hay net are also needed. Foodstuffs should be kept in vermin-proof containers with lids. You will save money by buying hay and straw in big quantities early in the season. If you have no barn or shed in which you can store them, stack them out of doors. This needs to be done carefully on dry ground. The stack should be covered with a weighted-down waterproof sheet. Make sure you have all you need to keep and look after a horse or pony before going out to buy one.

## Grooming

Grooming helps circulation and keeps the skin and coat in good condition. Stabled or partly stabled animals should be groomed thoroughly every day. Horses that are living outdoors, but are in work, should be groomed daily in the summer. In winter, they should be brushed over only to remove dirt and mud. Leave some grease in their coats to help keep them warm. Use the dandy brush for this. The body brush is the one that really cleans. The metal currycomb is designed to clean the brush as you work. The stable rubber gives a final polish. The hoof pick should be used regularly. The water brush and mane comb prepare the mane for pulling and braiding. Tail tangles should be worked free by hand and the tail should then be brushed out with the body brush.

Always keep a saddle on a rack or trestle. If you are setting it down anywhere other than the tack room, do so carefully with the pommel downward. Tack is expensive and should therefore be cared for and kept clean and in good repair. New saddles will need re-stuffing after about a year of use.

For your horse: mane comb, metal and rubber currycombs, body brush and dandy brush, hoof pick, halter, clip rope, saddle and bridle.

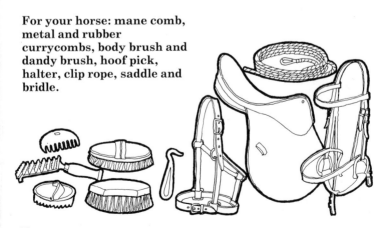

## Horse and Rider

The horse or pony you buy must suit your height and weight as well as your riding ability. All native ponies can carry a fair weight for their height. Welsh Cobs, Connemaras, Fells, Dales, and Highlands are all suitable for adults as well as for older children. If you are very tall you will need a horse of considerable height. If you are small, avoid buying one so tall that it is difficult to mount (it would also be difficult for you to groom it properly). If you are heavy, a cob type or a big native would suit you best. Many tall horses are not up to the weight of a good cob. A small, light adult has a wide choice. Long distance riding groups have no height limit. The most important factor when buying a pony is for the rider to feel happy and confident on it.

Wrong

Wrong

Right

**Right: The top two pictures show riders who are mounted on horses which are wrong for their size. Choose neither a big horse if you are small and light nor a small one if you are tall. You and your mount should match each other in build.**

63

# Buying a Horse or Pony

You should set out to buy a horse or pony with a good idea of the sort of animal you want, and what you can afford to pay. Do not be too fussy about color. There is an old saying which goes: "A good horse is never a bad color." Whether you buy a mare or a **gelding** is up to you but do not buy a young horse or pony for a child or a beginner. Only experienced riders can teach young animals their job. Older horses give confidence and prove to be the best "schoolmasters." Those that have been well cared for can stay sound and happy to work far into their twenties.

Advertisements in an equestrian magazine, or in the local paper often provide the first step. Make an appointment to see anything that seems suitable and if possible take a knowledge-able friend with you. If you have been having lessons, your riding school may be able to find what you want.

### Ask your Instructor

Your instructor is probably the best person to know exactly the type of horse you need. Also, it benefits their

**Above: Always let the seller or the seller's child ride first when buying. It is better that the horse buck them off than you.**

reputation to find a good match. A good way to find children's ponies is through the local pony club branch. Sooner or later all children outgrow their ponies and the pony club instructors will probably know the ponies' life histories.

Particularly with children's ponies, it is worth asking if you can have the pony for a trial period. It may seem a joy to ride at first, but half the pleasure of owning a pony comes from being able to handle it confidently and make a friend of it. Unless you are very knowledgeable it is unwise to buy at a sale.

## Advice from a Vet

Before you decide to buy a particular horse or pony, you should have it "vetted." This is when your veterinarian (not the seller's) checks that it is sound in "wind, eyes, limbs, and heart." He or she will also check its age, unless it is a registered animal with pedigree papers stating its year of birth. If all goes well you should not need the vet too often. Nonetheless, it is a good thing to get to know one. If you are a novice rider, contact him or her whenever you are even slightly doubtful about the health of your horse or pony. Keep the vet's telephone number in a handy place and remember that it is much better to make the phone call too early than too late.

**Below: Before buying a horse or pony, it is important to get it "vetted." Here, the veterinarian is checking the animal for soundness. First, the horse is ridden and then it will be checked for "heart and wind."**

**Above: New Zealand rug with surcingle (some modern ones are made to stay in place without it). Above right: Cozy quilted night rug (can also be wool-lined jute).**

## Blankets and Rugs

Native ponies should not need "blanketing," unless they are doing a lot of work in winter, and have to be clipped. There are three principal kinds of clip. The trace-clip takes hair off the belly, between the thighs and forearms, and up the underside of the neck. The hunter-clip takes hair off the whole body with the exception of a saddlepatch, the legs, and, usually, the head. The full-clip is only for horses in hard winter work (show jumpers on the winter indoor circuit, for example). Native ponies with a trace-clip can continue to live outdoors, but will need to wear New Zealand rugs in cold, wet, and windy weather. All other ponies that are trace-clipped can be kept out in New Zealand rugs by day but will probably need a night rug when brought in. In winter, a horse with a full-clip will need an under blanket (sometimes two) as well as a night rug. If it is turned out it will also need a rug under its New Zealand.

A cooler rug is useful to throw over horses or ponies that come in sweaty or soaked by rain. If the pony is really drenched, a layer of straw along its back under the rug will help it dry off. This is called thatching. If you go to shows, a cotton day sheet, worn in the stable beforehand and also when traveling, will help to keep the coat clean and lying flat. It is sensible to have a spare New Zealand rug. If one gets soaked, the other can be worn while it dries. Although native ponies do not need rugs, it is sensible to have one in case of illness.

## Company for Horses and Ponies

You should never forget that horses are herd animals. Their instinct is to roam freely in the company of their own kind. So by domesticating them we are asking them to live quite against their nature. Although some can become accustomed to living alone, the majority are happier with a companion.

This does not have to be another horse or pony. Stabled horses sometimes make good friends with the stable cat, allowing it to sleep curled up on their back. Some become friendly with goats, and most seem to like donkeys. The problem with donkeys is that they often catch lungworm, so a donkey companion needs to be

Above: A Connemara Pony in its native country. These versatile ponies are good mounts for both adults and children Most of them love jumping.

checked for this.

Stabled horses should be able to see each other and the yard. A single stabled horse will be happier if its stall is near the house so that it can watch everyone's daily activities. It is unnatural for a horse to spend long hours confined in even the largest stall. All stabled horses, should be turned out for at least a part of every day so that they can do what they like. If they want to buck or roll, they must be given the chance to do so.

# Your Pony's Health

When people talk about "stable vices" they mean one or other of three things: "crib-biting," "wind-sucking," or "weaving." These can all damage the health of the horse and so a seller should always state if an animal has any of these habits. Horses will copy one another. One crib-biter, wind-sucker, or weaver will soon have his friends doing the same thing.

A crib-biter bites the top of the stable door or any convenient wooden surface. At the same time it draws in air. This harms both its teeth and

**Above: A pony crib-biting. This is a habit usually caused by boredom. It is bad for the pony – and for the stable door!**

its digestion. A wind-sucker arches its neck and sucks in air which it then swallows. This is also very bad for digestion. When weaving, the horse sways from side to side the whole time he should be standing still. All three habits are mainly caused by boredom. Horses which are permanently stabled (or those who do not get enough exercise and attention) are more likely to develop these habits.

## First Aid

For first aid emergencies it is important to keep the following items in or near the stables: a mild disinfectant, an antiseptic powder, a healing ointment, a liniment, a tin of kaolin poultice, a tube of eye ointment, a thermometer, a pair of blunt-ended scissors, two crepe bandages and a roll of cotton.

Minor cuts and scratches can be treated by bathing them with mild disinfectant or salt water. Then they can be dusted with antiseptic powder. When the cuts or scratches have healed, smooth on ointment to soften the scar tissue and help the hair to grow again. Puncture wounds and deep cuts are more serious and you should call the vet. Never delay in calling him if an animal is lame, shows signs of ill health or has a rise of temperature. The normal temperature for a horse is 100°F (30°C). It is taken by inserting a greased thermometer into the rectum. Signs of ill health include coughs, runny noses, lack of energy, constipation, diarrhea, loss of appetite, a harsh coat, and a constant desire to roll (this is probably colic).

Follow the advice of the veterinarian carefully. If he says that you must rest the horse for three weeks, do not ride it in two weeks because "it seems all right." If your pony goes lame on a ride, do not panic! Lift the foot on which it is lame, to see if it has picked up a stone. This is a common cause of sudden lameness. If you remove the stone, the pony will generally recover right away.

If there is no stone, walk the pony home and (unless you have an experienced parent) ask your vet to come and see what is causing the lameness. He will tell you how to treat it.

**Below: All horses enjoy a good roll. If stabled horses are to be kept happy, it is necessary for them to have periods of freedom when they can gallop about, play together and roll to their heart's content.**

# Feeding

Horses are grazing animals. They have different feeding habits from meat-eaters. Grazers eat small amounts throughout the day. Their relatively small stomachs are designed to cope with this. It is important, therefore, to feed them as near as possible to their natural habits. Grass or hay (called bulk food) provides their main diet, and concentrates (energy foods) should be fed according to their work.

The amount of concentrate food a horse needs depends on the work it does, its temperament, and the ability of its rider. It is just as bad for them to be too fat as too thin so it is helpful to know the amount of food a horse needs in 24 hours. The total weight for a horse of 59 in. (150 cm or 15 hh) should not be more than 26 lb (12 kg). Add or subtract 1 lb (0.45 kg) for every 1 in. (2.5 cm) more or less of height. Of the 26 lb (12 kg) of food, if 6 lb (2.5 kg) is concentrate, then 20 lb (9 kg) bulk is required. The more concentrate, the less bulk is needed. Ponies need about

Oats are an energy-producing food. They should be fed bruised. Bran (powdery substance) is useful for making a mash. Pellets can be fed to ponies. Coarse mixes vary; read the details on the package before buying.

2lb (0.8kg) less weight per height.

It is hard to go far wrong if you stick to the weight for height guide. But horses, like humans, are individuals. Some need more food to keep in condition than others. Animals which are out at grass at night eat about 10lb. when the grass is good. In winter, the grass has little nutrition in it and even if the horse is out all day, it should have its full ration of hay.

## Rules for Feeding

A basic rule of feeding is "little and often." This applies to the concentrate feeds; each feed should not weigh more than 4lb. If a horse needs a lot of concentrate food, it should be given four feeds rather than one or two enormous ones. Overloading the stomach means that it can no longer pass the food through to the intestines for digestion. The result is colic.

Another feeding rule is "do not work the horse on a full stomach." Allow it an hour or two for digestion before strenuous work and a little less before gentle hacking. A full stomach looks swollen. It presses on the lungs and makes it difficult for the horse to breathe. If water is always available horses will not drink too much or at the wrong time. Try to encourage your pony to have a drink on the way in from a ride before it is fed.

## Types of Feed

Oats, barley, corn, cubes, and some coarse mixes are energy-giving concentrates. The most nutritious one is oats. Oats can make horses too excitable for novice riders. It should not normally be fed to children's ponies. Cubes or a coarse mix or flaked barley are best. Boiled whole barley mixed with bran makes a good winter feed. Corn should not be fed on its own as it lacks fiber. Coarse mixes vary but the good brands will say on the sack which mix is best for which kind of work.

Mixes with a lot of corn are best fed in winter. Bran is useful to make mashes. A little added to feeds encourages the horse to eat more slowly. Sugar beet (cubes and pulp) is a good appetizer and conditioner, but it must be soaked before feeding. It can be fed all year. Linseed is good if you are trying to get some shine on your horse's coat. Never feed your horse cattle cubes or mixes.

## Hay

There are four main kinds of hay: seed, meadow, timothy, and clover. All good hay should smell sweet. An opened bale should fall apart in slices, as it went into the baler. Seed and meadow hay are a green/fawn color; timothy is yellower and clover is darker. Old horses find seed or meadow hay easier to chew than timothy. Seed and timothy are the most usual types of hay but horses like meadow hay especially. It is also very good for them. Clover hay is difficult to make well.

Different hays vary in weight. Clover is the heaviest, next comes timothy, then seeds and finally meadow. When you buy a batch of hay, it is a good plan to weigh a full net on a hanging scale so you know how much you are feeding. With practice you can soon judge weight without weighing. Whatever the total amount you are feeding, most of it should be given at night. If you shake the slices out with a pitchfork before filling the hay net, this loosens the hay and shakes out any dust. It also makes it easier to fill the nets, and easier for the horse to pull the hay out.

If there is no running water in a field, the horse will need a drinking trough. The trough must be kept both clean and full, and in winter make sure the ice gets broken. Stable water buckets should be solid and kept in place in a corner of the stable

**Left: Always tie a hay net with a slip-knot or you will find it difficult to untie. Pass the tie rope through one of the lower meshes to ensure that the net does not fall too low as it empties.**

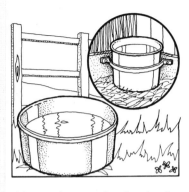

**Above: A water bucket in the corner of a box can be held in place with a hoop of wire or positioned behind a straight strip of wood. Water containers in fields should be kept clean and filled.**

and well-kept to be any good at all. One large field is best used by dividing it into sections. This can be done with an electric fence which allows one part to be grazed while another is limed or fertilized. In small fields, droppings should be picked up as often as possible. If a field has ragwort it should be dug up, removed and burned. Check that there are no poisonous plants or trees in the area. Some common ones are yew, rhododendrons, and mistletoe.

behind a bar or strip of wood. These should also be kept clean along with the mangers, feed pans or buckets. Take any movable feeding utensils out of the box when the horse has finished, or it will amuse itself by kicking them around. Clean out any food left in the manger, feed pan or bucket before offering the fresh feed.

The best but most expensive fencing is made with posts and rails. Wire is acceptable provided it is kept taut and the posts are firm. Do not use barbed wire. Hedges must be thick, old,

**Above: The owner of this horse allowed the hedge of his field to become thin and the wooden fence to break down. Even posts and rails fall into disrepair. It is important to keep hedges and fences in good repair if you want to prevent your pony disappearing into the distance!**

# Showing and Competing

Allow plenty of time before a show for grooming your horse or pony. Gray ones will need stable stains and grass stains washed off. But remember that too much shampooing of the whole animal is bad for its skin. Energetic grooming with the body brush puts coats in peak condition. Finish off the grooming by rubbing over with a folded stable rubber. If the animal normally lives outdoors, keep it stabled the night before the show if at all possible. Wash its mane, tail, white socks or stockings and be sure to dry these out thoroughly. Stable bandages help to keep white socks or stockings clean. A cotton day sheet left on overnight will keep the coat clean and lying flat.

**Below: On fine days, it is pleasant to groom out of doors.**

**Above: It is not easy to pull or braid a mane. Ask a friend to show you how the first time.**

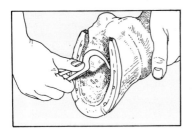

**Above: When picking out a hoof start at the heel and remember to clean the cleft of the frog.**

**Above: Hoof oil looks nice and is good for the hoof. Paint well up into the coronet.**

Apart from native ponies and Arabs, all ponies and horses should be shown with their manes pulled and braided for hunter, jumper, and dressage classes. Their tails, too, should be pulled or braided, and neatly banged at the bottom to the length, between hock and fetlock, that suits the animal best. It is not easy either to pull or braid a mane. Try to get a knowledgeable friend to show you how and practice braiding a few times before you do it for the show. Braids should be sewn rather than bound with a rubber band. The same applies to pulling, or braiding, tails. It is easy to make a mess of the job. Shoes should have been checked about a week before the show. If new ones are needed, the animal will have time to get used to them. Keep the feet very clean and oil the hooves regularly. Remember to take hoof oil with you to the show. Some of the braids put in the night before may need tightening in the morning, so give yourself time.

The basic requirements for traveling are methods of leg and tail protection. Legs should either be bandaged, or the pony should wear one of the modern "leg protectors." Bandages should have cotton wool under them. A tail bandage stops the tail from getting rubbed. Do not bandage below the dock (the bone of the tail). Instead, finish near the top with a bow or double bow to the outside. It is sensible to put valuable animals into knee caps and hock boots. Buckle the top strap to fit the leg and leave the lower one more loose. Make sure that the buckles remain on the outside. If the animal wears a tail guard it must also wear a rug, as one end of the guard is fixed through the rug's **surcingle**.

A leather **halter** is better for traveling than one made of nylon. If a horse pulls back or gets upset, leather will break. It can practically hang itself with unbreakable nylon. In winter, a night rug can be worn for traveling, although this will depend on the vehicle. Some trailers become quite hot and a cotton sheet might be enough. In summer, the cotton day sheet which keeps the coat clean and the tail guard should be all that is needed. Take a cooler with you for good measure and never travel with the horse "tacked up."

Even if your horse is an experienced traveler, practice loading it a few times before a show. The whole procedure can be made easier by putting a feed in the van or trailer. If the horse is an "awkward loader," try to stand the vehicle in a place where one side of the ramp is guarded by a wall or gate. Make sure the animal can see right into the inside. Walk with the horse toward and up the ramp as far as it

**This horse is prepared for traveling with hock boots, knee caps, bandages, a cotton day sheet and a tail guard.**

**Above: A horse is about to be loaded into a horse box. It is wearing a day rug, traveling bandages from knee and hock to coronet and overreach boots to protect the heels of the fore feet.**

will go. If it stops, do not turn around at it or pull it; instead, get your helper to give it a gentle shove.

Always make sure that the ramp is steady. Once inside the van, the helper does up the backstrap and puts up the ramp while you tie the horse with a slip knot. Make sure you have a thoughtful driver. An uncomfortable ride can sometimes turn a horse into

an "awkward loader." When unloading go quietly to the front and hold the animal while the helper lets down the ramp and releases the backstrap.

**Preparing for a Show**
Prepare everything you need for the show the night before. Remember your grooming kit, hoof oil, needle and thread (in case a braid comes out on the way), a cooler, a bucket for water, and a feed for your mount. If you plan to jump as well as show, take whatever boots or bandages you need. Tie a filled hay net in the van or trailer. On the actual day allow yourself

plenty of time to park, unload, and prepare your mount. Give it a final polish and remember to re-oil the hooves.

If you are involved in only one class but you still want to see the rest of the show, remember to look after your horse. Untack it, offer it water, put on its cooler, and tie it to the side of the trailer with a hay net. If you have a van, return the horse to it with a supply of hay. Do not use your mount as a "grandstand" for the day. If you have a jumping or working hunter class later, you could give it a small feed.

Get ready in good time for a jumping or working hunter class. You may need to put on **over-reach boots**, leg bandages or boots, and you will

**Above: Between classes, horses can be tied to the side of a box or trailer with hay nets. The horse on the left is wearing a cotton day sheet and the one on the right wears an anti-sweat rug.**

probably want to go over the practice jump. Try not to overdo this. There is no point in exhausting your mount before the competition begins.

Canter around in the practice arena trying to get the horse working well, then try the jump three or four times. If the horse jumps fluently, praise it well. Then go back to working on the flat with a little free walk on a long rein. If you like, have one more jump before going into the ring, but do not let people tempt you to be competitive in the practice arena.

## Walking the Course

Riders do not walk the course to see how high the jumps are. They look, instead, at the angles at which they are set. Then they work out the best line of approach and pace it. Try to work out which jumps may pose the biggest problem, Count the distance in strides between each part of a double or triple. It is important to walk the course intelligently before your jumping class. This will avoid asking the impossible of your mount. That can happen by turning into a jump at an angle which is too sharp or by not allowing time to recover balance and attention before one of the awkward ones.

It is usual to show horses in double bridles, although four-year-olds and working hunters can be shown in snaffles. Ponies with small mouths are correct in pelhams (with two reins). It is not correct to show in a martingale. For jumping, you can use any bit, bridle, or martingale you like.

Below: The line-up of prize-winning riding ponies at a big show. Notice how neatly the children are turned out. The ponies are beautiful too and have been trained to stand quietly and squarely.

Once tacked up, ride in quietly and be prepared to go into the warm-up ring when your class is called. The calmer you can keep yourself beforehand, the more sensibly your mount is likely to behave. Say hello to any friends you may see, but do not let them distract.

**Below: Once an animal has been taken out of the van it is important to keep it covered with a sheet before it has to compete. This pony's young rider is braiding its mane, having brought the animal water in the white container and provided it with a hay net. The red and black silks on the skull cap in the drawer are the colors the rider will wear.**

## Competing

Once inside the warm-up ring, pay attention to your riding and try to get the co-operation of your mount. In the ring itself you will circle in a clockwise direction, first at walk, then at trot, then at canter. You may be asked to "change the rein" (go the other way around). When riding, try neither to mask another rider nor get yourself blocked in. If you want to pass someone, do so on a bend. In Britain, when everyone has returned to a walk, the custom is for the judge to tell the steward the order in which the riders are to be called into line. At this point, watch for the steward's signal. Then walk to the place directed and stand quietly until the line is complete.

Each horse and rider will then be asked to give an individual show. This will involve a trot and canter on each rein. Then comes a halt, and if your mount can, a few steps of rein back. Do not make this too long. All the judges want to see is that your mount goes freely, canters on either lead and halts obediently. The simplest way of doing this is with a neat figure eight at trot and canter. You may then be

**Above: This rider is walking the horse quietly round the ground at a show. This helps to accustom it to its surroundings.**

asked to unsaddle and show your mount "in hand." If so, lead it out to stand in front of the judge, then walk away and trot back. A friend can come into the ring to help you unsaddle and tack up again.

Once everyone has re-mounted you will probably walk around again before the final placings. Judges often change their opinions when they have seen animals without their saddles. Rosette winners do a lap of honor.

# Club Competitions

Riding clubs and pony clubs run many interesting competitions. Combined training is dressage with jumping. Horse trials are one day events. Hunter trials are purely cross-country rides. All are run at different levels to suit every kind of horse and rider. Below the elementary stage, all dressage tests must be ridden in a snaffle (except for some pony club ones, when you may use a pelham). Neither martingales, nor boots and bandages are allowed on the horse. For cross-country, as for show jumping, more or less any bit, bridle, martingale or noseband is permitted. But you must wear a skull cap, and it is usual to ride in a sweatshirt or sweater which matches the color of the silks on your cap.

It is vital to spend time walking the cross-country course to fix it in your mind. This makes sure you know which jumps are in your section. It is also important to work out if there are easier alternatives and to decide whether or not to take them. Try to note the position of the direction flags. You can be disqualified for going the wrong side of one. It is tempting, at a show, to be sidetracked socializing with friends but, as you can see, there is a great deal to do first.

Every course has a time limit. If you exceed it you will get time penalties. Do not worry about this. It is better to aim for a safe, clear round than risk coming to grief by going too fast. Gymkhana games are fun and need a fast, handy obedient mount rather than a show pony.

**Left: A prizewinner is doing a "lap of honor" at a show. She is under 16, and so she is wearing jodhpur boots. These look very neat. Right: Young riders ready to compete on well-groomed ponies.**

# Showing in Hand

Horses and ponies under four years are shown "in hand." An animal should not be grossly fat for these classes but it should be well-fleshed. Its quarters should be rounded and its neck strong and muscled. Its coat should be sleek and glossy, and its outlook alert. It should be healthy, lively, and strong muscled. To produce a youngster in show condition, it is not necessary to feed it large quantities of oats. This might make it over-excitable in the ring. Flaked barley, some sugar beet, maybe a little corn and some linseed mashes will do the trick.

If an animal is to be shown early in the year and you want to shed its winter coat, try keeping it in at night. Blanket it and give it regular daily grooming sessions. Native ponies are best shown later when their summer coats are through.

If a youngster is to show successfully it must be taught show manners. It must lead well at walk and trot and stand square when asked. When led it should move freely, level with your shoulder. Avoid holding the lead rein or reins too close to the bridle or halter. Wear comfortable shoes so that you can really run when asked to trot. When you are asked to walk away and trot

**Left: This young rider has been lucky enough to win a red rosette which is just visible on the pony's bridle. After using all that energy, now it is time for the pony to have a rest and for the rider to sit back and relax.**

back to the judge, turn yourself around your exhibit rather than turn it around you. When asked to stand square, stand in front of your animal and try to keep it looking alert. You can do this by feeling in your pockets for tidbit or even by picking a bit of grass. Carry a short crop and be neat and tidily dressed and groomed yourself.

To show a mare and foal, teach the foal to lead and get a friend to help you on the day. **Yearlings** can be shown in halters without a bit. As they get older they are easier to control wearing a plain unjointed snaffle buckled on to a show halter. A white

**Above: When showing a pony in hand you must try to run as energetically as the pony to show it off to best effect. Remember to wear comfortable shoes or boots in which you can run easily.**

lead rein always looks nice. A touch of petroleum jelly around the eyes and nostrils brightens up the appearance and a little methylated spirit on a cloth rubbed over the coat will remove any lingering dust. All native ponies should be shown with natural manes and tails, but you can tidy these if they are very uneven and shampoo them until they are soft and silky.

85

## After the Show

After a show or competition your horse or pony deserves to rest. It will appreciate a bran mash before its regular feed. If it lives outdoors, give the mash in a loose box. Check that the horse is cool and calm before you turn it out.

If you stable the horse, bed it deeply and leave it with mash, water, and hay. When you settle it for the night, give it a regular feed. After a strenuous competition, rest it the next day and if it is stabled turn it out for at least part of the day.

When you are very young, you probably enjoy the fun of gymkhana games. As you get

**Below: Back home, the pony should be fed and made warm and comfortable in its box. When its feed pan is removed it will probably lie down and rest.**

older you learn to appreciate the excitement of competitive riding. By fifty, you will probably find that it is not necesary to be continually jumping obstacles and going fast to enjoy riding. You may already have become interested in dressage. At this point, you will have time to take it more seriously. You can work on perfecting your own riding because with dressage your competitive days will certainly not be over.

Mrs. Lorna Johnstone was 70 when she represented Great Britain at the Mexico Olympics in 1972. She finished 12th, which at that

**Above: Here is Mrs. Jennie Loriston Clarke performing dressage on her stallion *Dutch Courage*. Until the horse retired in 1985, these two were a most successful and popular dressage partnership. Dressage may be slower than eventing but it is just as competitive.**

time was the highest placed British Olympic dressage rider ever. Riding is the one sport which you can enjoy and go on perfecting all your life, and dressage is the one discipline in which age is no disadvantage.

# Riding for Fun

It may be exciting to compete and fun to show, but you should try never to get too competition-minded. Even worse are those people who immediately want a new horse or pony if they do not win enough with the old one. If you want to ride, it should be because you like horses and ponies. You should not ride just because it gives you a chance to show off.

Riding at any level is a partnership between two living creatures. The better we understand our horses and ponies, the closer the partnership and the more we will enjoy our riding. Horses are individuals and each has a character of its own. They may not be allowed inside the house like other pets, but they are just as ready to become friends with humans as cats and dogs.

Riding is not just a competitive sport. Many riders get as much pleasure out of a restful day in the country as they do out of competitions. In fact, some people enjoy riding precisely because it allows them the chance to explore the beautiful countryside around them. Riding around in the company of a horse or pony reminds riders that they too are part of the natural world.

To own a horse or pony is a pleasure, but it is also a responsibility. Dogs and cats can run off and scavenge or find a new home. Horses and ponies rely totally on their owners for health and, in some cases, survival. If we forget to feed or water them, they go hungry and thirsty. If we stable them with no bedding they cannot lie down and rest. If, in winter, we turn them out in a field with no shelter, they will be cold and miserable. So, whether they win us prizes and glory or not, it is still up to us to care for them as best we can, "through sickness and in health."

**In today's busy world, it is restful and enjoyable to forget the stress of competitions for a day. To explore the country in the company of a horse or pony reminds the rider that he, too, is part of the natural world.**

# Glossary

**Aids** The ways in which a rider communicates his wishes to the horse or pony when riding.

**Bone** The measurement around the cannon bone taken just below the knee. (A horse with " good bone" has a measurement of between $8\frac{1}{2}$ and $9\frac{1}{2}$ inches (21 cm and 24 cm) and is capable of carrying more weight than one that is light of bone).

**Broken to saddle** Is the term applied to a young horse which has completed its initial training.

**Cannon Bone** The bone between knee, hock, and fetlock joint.

**Cantle** The back of the saddle.

**Carnivores** Animals which feed on flesh or other animal matter.

**Cob** A horse or pony with a particular kind of conformation: a well-rounded rib cage, a compact body, well-rounded and muscular quarters, relatively short legs with good bone and therefore strong and up to weight.

**Colt** An uncastrated male horse under four years old.

**Coronet** The point at which the foot joins the hoof.

**Dorsal stripe** A dark stripe running along the spine of many native ponies.

**Dressage** Training of a horse in obedience and deportment.

**Equine** All horses are equines, just as all cats are felines.

**Extinct** A term applied to a species when it has completely died out.

**Fetlock** The joint below the cannon bone and above the pastern.

**Filly** A female horse under four years old.

**Gelding** A castrated male horse.

**Halter** A piece of equipment worn on the head of the horse. It is made out of leather or nylon and enables you to tie the horse in the stable or in a van for traveling.

**Handicap** Races which are handicapped are those in which certain competitors are given extra weight to carry to make the contest more even.

**Herbivores** Animals which feed on plants.

**Hock** The joint at the top of the cannon bone on the hind leg.

**Incisors** Front cutting teeth.

**Jousting** A sport popular in the Middle Ages. Knights in full armor charged at one another with long spear-like sticks while riding on horseback.

**Mare** Female horse.

**Martingale** Prevents horses head rising too high. (1) Running – fixed to the reins; (2) Standing – fixed to the noseband.

**Molars** The back teeth of a horse (and other mammals) used for grinding.

**Muzzle** The lowest part of the horse's head including its nose and mouth.

**On the leg** Horse appearing to have too little body bulk for its length of leg.

**Over-reach boots** Boots worn by the horse on its forelegs when it jumps. They are designed to prevent the toe of the hind foot catching the heel of the forefoot when landing.

**Pampas** Grassy plains in South America.

**Passage** An advanced dressage movement. It is a collected trot in which the knees and hocks of the horse are raised high.

**Pastern** The part of the leg between fetlock joint and hoof composed of a number of small bones.

**Pelham** Bridle which combines curb and snaffle.

**Piaffe** A difficult dressage movement in which the horse does a rhythmic collected trot in place.

**Pirouette** A dressage movement performed at walk or canter. The horse moves the forehand around the quarters in a small full circle.

**Pommel** Upward projecting front part of the saddle.

**School figures** Movements practiced in an indoor school or outdoor arena.

**Shy** A sudden jump to the side by the horse (usually caused by an unexpected movement or noise).

**Silks** The colored covering put over skull caps or crash helmets by jockeys and cross-country riders.

**Skull cap** Protective head gear.

**Snaffle** A bit which can be jointed or unjointed.

**Stallion** An uncastrated male horse over four years.

**Stud farms** Places where horses are kept for breeding.

**Surcingle** A strap which keeps the rug in place.

**Tundras** Treeless Arctic regions in which the subsoil is frozen.

**Withers** The ridge between the shoulders of a horse.

**Yearling** Colt or filly between one and two years old.

# Index

Page numbers in *italics* refer to illustrations